RISING PHOENIX

A Practical Guide on How to Create the Life You Want, Through Transformation and Rebirth

DANIELLE RAMIREZ

Phoenix Rising Coaching Services, LLC

Contents

Acknowledgments	ix
Introduction	xv
1. Finding Your Self-Worth	1
2. The Perfect Relationship	7
3. Setting Boundaries	14
4. It Shouldn't Be This Hard	21
5. Speak it, Write it, Feel it!	28
6. Find Your Tribe, You'll Need Them	36
7. Who Are You? Really?	42
8. Say NO to Doubt	49
9. Stay True to You	56
10. Growth	62
Epilogue	69
About the Author	71

PHOENIXRISINGCOACHINGSERVICES, LLC

Published by Phoenix Rising Coaching Services, LLC

Copyright 2021 by Danielle Ramirez.

All rights reserved. No part of this book may be scanned, uploaded, reproduced, distributed, or transmitted in any form or by any means whatsoever without written permission from the author, except in the case of brief quotations embodied in critical articles and reviews. Thank you for supporting the author's rights.

For permission requests, please email the author at Support@phoenixrisingcoachingservices.com

First Printing June 2021

ISBN: 9781737533306

Disclaimer

The publisher and the author make no guarantees concerning the level of success you may experience by following the advice and strategies contained in this book, and you accept the risk that results will differ for each individual. The testimonials and examples provided in this book show exceptional results, which may not apply to the average reader, and are not intended to represent or guarantee that you will achieve the same or similar results.

This book is dedicated to

The little girl or little boy inside of our adult bodies that no one ever sees. Who looks for the golden ticket in every interaction. Who searches for happiness in all the wrong places, only to realize true happiness lies within.

When you read this book, I hope you find your happiness. Bask in it and know you are the only one who can create it. Find your purpose and know you are the only one who can excel from it. Find yourself and know that as you read my story, you are creating your own and I can't wait to read it. ~

"You have to love yourself for who you are in all forms; otherwise you just exist instead of living."

- Danielle Ramirez, M.S. ACC

Acknowledgments

Thank you to:

God, The Universe, the Divine, and My Tribe;
Freddy, my husband who motivates me and inspires me to be great.

To Family and Friends, from my Past, Present, and my Future.

To my Phoenix Rising supporters: my editor Debbie Burke, and book cover designers Donna Lynn & Bruce Hall. Thank you for seeing my vision and bringing it to life.

"We cannot create the life we desire, unless we transform the behavior that no longer serves us. That is when true rebirth takes place."

- Danielle Ramirez M.S. ACC

"If you're not excited about the person you are, now is the time to get excited."

- Danielle Ramirez

Introduction

When you inspire yourself, others are inspired by you.

December 31, 1983 was the day I was born. December 31, 2019, the day I turned 36, was the day I finally gave life to who I was born to be. This has been a long time coming - according to the universe. It just took a global pandemic to speed up the process. I like to call COVID-19 a blessing in disguise. At 36 I told myself that I was ready to live on my own terms, and mainly, I wanted to find myself. I was tired of living for others and I wanted to know what life was really like living for myself.

Why now? Well, this book is about coming into the "you" phase. I had been through a lot during my 36 years here in the universe and up until this point, I had no idea who I was as a woman, entrepreneur nor a wife. I was determined to live MY life as I saw fit. Women put so much pressure on themselves to rise to every occasion except for the main one, the occasion for self. I was one of those women. I would worry about how I was viewed amongst my peers, family and coworkers. It was like playing a role in other people's screenplay, while my character was constantly changing. I played these different versions

Introduction

of who I pretended to be all to keep certain people in my life. I literally was wearing a mask since the age of eight years old and this character, the people-pleaser, was one of the hardest characters to live up to.

Up until the age of 36, I was broken. I have to say, the universe forced me to place the puzzle pieces in the right places, instead of forcing pieces in areas that didn't fit. The following guide has helped me rediscover myself, break generational cycles and establish better relationships in a way that only I could. I hope that through my experiences, you can find yourself and know that it's always okay to put yourself first.

1

Finding Your Self-Worth

"Nothing changes, unless something changes."

I read somewhere that the spiritual meaning of the number 36 is to focus less on the material perspectives and more on your profound life. The moment I turned 36, I felt an overwhelming shift to break a cycle of regret and to adopt a pattern of living and learning. I started having important conversations with myself. I knew I wasn't happy; I knew I had to find a way to find my peace. I grew up seeking maternal love. They say that the first people you ever fall in love with are your mother and father. I believe that we also grow up placing images on people expecting them to fulfill a void that we lack from our childhood. Our relationships are a direct reflection of what we seek within ourselves. When I lost my father at eight years old, I had to understand pain, love, grief and emptiness all while still just being a little girl.

When you experience loss, especially at a young age, you realize that life doesn't come easily, especially when it hits you like a ton of bricks. I found my self-worth by understanding and embracing that eight-year-old child who sought love through a traumatic event that still felt raw. I spoke with her (me) daily. I encouraged her to say what she felt. She had been hiding for so long behind temper tantrums, hurt, and pain; I could see she needed love.

I began to say those very words to her, "You matter," "You are loved," "I am here for you," and started the path to healing. When she cried, I consoled her, when she wanted to play, I did something fun. I knew that the first step to healing was to heal her.

Women come with a lot of layers, but within those layers, your voice can be found. I learned three things that can bring your healing into alignment: understand your trauma, embrace your trauma and recover from your trauma. When you choose healing, you are choosing to acknowledge both the broken parts and the parts that have healed along the way. You understand the power of forgiveness and learn that validation is needed from no one other than yourself.

It's important to look at whatever it is in your life that has been difficult to bear as a mirror to readjust, refocus and change the pattern. Childhood traumas are real and set the foundation for us into adulthood. The level of vulnerability that comes with healing is surreal. Picture a double mirror, one of life as a child and the other as an adult. Are we mirroring our childhood or are we mirroring a life that we set out for ourselves to reach our truest potential?

Everyone has obstacles and everyone also has milestones. The rewarding part is knowing that you have control and choices with both. We all desire to be something and what we think about, we attract into our lives. Create a balance between your mind and experiences, and you will have the perfect harmony.

REFLECTION QUESTION #1
WHAT IS SOMETHING I LEARNED ABOUT MYSELF THIS WEEK?

REFLECTION QUESTION # 2
GROWTH AND SELF-ESTEEM. WHAT DO THOSE WORDS MEAN TO YOU?

_____
_____
_____
_____
_____
_____
_____
_____
_____
_____
_____
_____
_____
_____
_____
_____
_____
_____
_____
_____
_____
_____
_____
_____

REFLECTION QUESTION #3
WHAT DO YOU ADMIRE MOST ABOUT YOURSELF?

_____
_____
_____
_____
_____
_____
_____
_____
_____
_____
_____
_____
_____
_____
_____
_____
_____
_____

DANIELLE RAMIREZ

2

The Perfect Relationship

"In a world of lost souls, don't become one."

Some may say there is no such thing as the "perfect relationship." I am here to say that there is such a thing because I have experienced it. Getting to know who you are is the most wonderful relationship that you can explore. You are in charge. You are the first to experience your growth and you are the only one who can truly reflect on your life in a positive way. Take my experience, for example - suffocating is the best way I can describe how I was feeling in my life when it came to pleasing people.

Doing some deep reflections on my life thus far helped me realize a few key points: (1) I was not putting myself first, and (2) I was focused on pleasing others. I realized that when you start to grow into who you are and discover that a part of your trauma is a lack of love, you'll realize that you've been searching for love in all the wrong places. I focused on pleasing others because I thought seeing others happy gave me a sense of happiness. However, what most people don't realize is that when we continue to please others, we are never truly pleasing them, we are just pacifying them. We can't save nor please anyone.

Women are natural nurturers and healers of the planet. Society has placed unrealistic expectations on women as a gender to please and take care of everyone. Yet, instead, we should be nurturing, healing and caring for ourselves first. With that realization, I learned about the perfect relationship. Layer by layer I rid parts of me that created stagnation, doubt, and fear. I learned that the perfect relationship begins with self. If you have had trauma in your life, learn to transmute that into motivation, confidence, and trust. Those very steps encouraged me to, at my own pace, break away from pleasing people and to have the greatest relationship with myself that was consistent and filled with patience, understanding and love.

I wanted bigger and better for myself, and I knew I had the opportunity to create it because I believed in myself. Now, fear, doubt, and stagnation still existed, but the difference is, when those feelings came, I acknowledged and identified where they were coming from and worked through them. It took lots of self-care that involved shadow work and inner-child healing to lead me to where I desired to be. I felt a huge block and was compelled to blame others for my shortcomings when it was just all the energy I allowed to consume and control me over the years.

Not having a good relationship with yourself is almost compared to being stagnant and stuck in a lost reality. If you ever get the feeling that you can't prosper in your current situation, then you are being controlled by your current situation. In most cases, we are the ones holding ourselves back. I became unapologetic, not wanting to apologize or explain myself anymore for my actions or moves. I was empowered. I wanted to feel powerful and more in control of how I felt.

Looking at my day-to-day activities, I realized that I was being micromanaged by people in my life and didn't even know it.

If you pay attention to the patterns of your life, you'll begin to realize everything revolves around energy. The feeling of not having a true sense of self-worth and empowerment will deeply reflect in your everyday life and relationships, but once we change the pattern, the outcome will start to reveal itself. The door that opened for me was to set the goal of acceptance and redirection to bring balance. There comes a time where you may feel unsure if you can take back control, when not having any is all you've ever known. Sometimes, what's comfortable and familiar is not always good for you. There's a sense of balance and peace when it comes to setting realistic goals for yourself. This process allows you to reclaim your power in making decisions that are within your highest good and that fall in line with your purpose and path. Look at yourself in the mirror and ask yourself, are you in control or are you being controlled? Your answer should lead you on a path to creating change and amplifying it.

People will always try and place a certain level of expectation on you. This is a form of control. You have the choice to live up to those expectations or you can create and stand on your own. When you choose the path of least resistance (Self), you begin to discover that through love, light and wisdom, your only power is to own and acknowledge every part of you, with grace.

DANIELLE RAMIREZ

REFLECTION QUESTION #1
WHAT ARE MY BIGGEST STRENGTHS?

_____
_____
_____
_____
_____
_____
_____
_____
_____
_____
_____
_____
_____
_____
_____
_____
_____
_____
_____
_____
_____

REFLECTION QUESTION # 2
WHAT CAN I DO TO NOURISH THE EXISTING RELATIONSHIP WITH MYSELF?

_____
_____
_____
_____
_____
_____
_____
_____
_____
_____
_____
_____
_____
_____
_____
_____
_____
_____
_____
_____
_____
_____

REFLECTION QUESTION # 3
WHAT IS ONE COMPLIMENT I WOULD GIVE MYSELF? WHY?

Rising Phoenix

3

Setting Boundaries

"Boundaries are your BEST Friend."

Setting boundaries can be a challenge. Trust me I know. Boundaries can make or break certain relationships, even the one with yourself. If you don't have set boundaries with others and yourself, get some. First step to setting boundaries is acknowledging that you probably have none. Prime example, do people just call you at any time for anything? Do people just invite themselves in your space? Are you allowing others to treat you less than you deserve? Chances are if the answers to any of these questions are "yes," then you need more stable boundaries and that's okay. You're about to set some.

First step to setting boundaries is starting with setting some with yourself. If you can't control your environment internally, you won't be able to control it externally. This involves learning and listening to your body. My body used to feel exhausted, I would go from experiencing headaches to just shutting down when I was in certain environments. I remember there would be times I would go to events with people just to please them, when in reality I never wanted to be there in the first place. I was committed to people pleasing again and I would fight against pleasing myself only to feel extremely tired and depleted in the end. I never felt secure in speaking up for myself because I was too concerned about what others may think. I realized that again, that it was related to trauma that I had carried along the way. Not using your voice when it comes to boundaries can make the mark when it comes to dealing with certain behaviors. If you won't speak up for yourself, who will?

Being able to recognize when your boundaries have been crossed and how they affect you is another aspect of learning how to establish and enforce them. If your mood declines due to certain behaviors being committed, chances are, this is a boundary issue for you. It's important to see how your mind, body and soul react to people, places and things, so that there is room to respond accordingly and remain grounded. Maintaining balance in grounding can help you focus, react accordingly and have a clearer mind when dealing with unacceptable behaviors.

TESTIMONY

WHAT IS A BOUNDARY, really? Some may think of it as a limitation while others may think of it as an opportunity to place standards in their lives. For me it is both. There was a time where I had no boundaries and I would allow people to take advantage of me. In reality, people were treating me how I treated myself. I decided to treat myself better and set some self-boundaries. Self-boundaries are boundaries where you set standards for yourself on how you treat yourself.

I was so confused on how I could blame others for how

they treated me when, yes, they were jerks for their wrongdoings, but I ultimately allowed it. I didn't talk to myself nicely or tell myself I love myself and I didn't take care of my mind, body and soul. Mostly, I didn't respect myself. I was feeding myself LIES!! In order for me to appreciate my future, I had to take a valuable lesson from my past. Do unto yourself, and attract what you deserve. I began to speak to myself with compassion, love and understanding. I sat in stillness with the fact that, for years, I had self-sabotaged my life by how I perceived myself.

My process for setting up boundaries involved and evolved around how much more love I had to give myself than I did others. I started to trust myself again with making decisions, mistakes and wise choices that impacted my life. I gave myself permission to just be. I also learned that no one can truly love you better than you love yourself, and when you start prioritizing yourself first, you will stop living your life for others and also be in perfect alignment and harmony with self.

Before now, I never understood the meaning behind "you can't love others unless you love yourself first." I thought that concept was unrealistic. But in the spirit of honesty and truth, what is unrealistic is placing obligation and holding others responsible for your happiness. It's not their job nor theirs to own. If you give others power to your happiness, you also give others power to your sadness.

REFLECTION QUESTION # 1
WHAT BOUNDARIES HAVE YOU SET FOR YOURSELF THIS YEAR?

_____
_____
_____
_____
_____
_____
_____
_____
_____
_____
_____
_____
_____
_____
_____
_____
_____
_____
_____
_____

REFLECTION QUESTION # 2
HOW CAN I CONTROL MY SELF-TALK WHEN I EXPERIENCE A BOUNDARY ISSUE?

_____
_____
_____
_____
_____
_____
_____
_____
_____
_____
_____
_____
_____
_____
_____
_____
_____
_____
_____
_____
_____
_____
_____

REFLECTION QUESTION # 3
DO YOU KNOW YOUR BOUNDARY CHALLENGES? IF SO, WHAT ARE THEY?

_____
_____
_____
_____
_____
_____
_____
_____
_____
_____
_____
_____
_____
_____
_____
_____
_____
_____
_____
_____
_____
_____
_____
_____
_____

DANIELLE RAMIREZ

4

It Shouldn't Be This Hard

"Be so inspired and focused on practicing gratitude that there is little room for negativity to render."

Staying in your head too long can be bad for your mental and physical health. I remember a time when I wouldn't finish important projects because I was in my head too long. It was all because I doubted myself. I asked my husband daily if I could write a book or start a business and be successful at it. I knew I had the skills, but needed some outside confirmation. Until one day, I had a long talk with my husband telling him I was regretting quitting my 9-5 job and scared of success and failure at the same time. I went into this long story about how during my childhood I wasn't told enough by the people who mattered the most, that I was good enough.

Remember in Step 1, we spoke about having deep conversations with self? Well, my inner child was all over this. I realized that although I was not given the confirmation that I was good enough, through my traumatic experiences, I was being prepared for the life I wanted and didn't even know it. I was given skills of perseverance, which gave me the ability not only to know that there was nothing wrong with me but also to connect my positive and negative experience to reclaim control. I made it through stages in life at a young age that would have had some people tapping out. For example, acknowledging and dealing with my negative experience of grief and loss as a child prepared me to understand and work through any negative experiences I dealt with later in life. I went from going to war with the US Army and dealing with multiple levels of trauma to learning how to create positive coping skills and eventually obtaining two college degrees, something I never thought that I could do.

Self-doubt held me back from understanding my worth. Knowing I was worth more than what I was receiving from others gave me the motivation to move forward and toward my dreams. Avoiding your experiences can hold you back from succeeding in life and put you on a roller coaster of emotions. What I have found helpful is to start journaling my thoughts. Journaling is a journey into how you think about yourself. For me, creating this book was my journal. I realized that I can't help someone navigate a path I never traveled on.

We are our worst inner critic and to be honest, life shouldn't be this hard. But we make it hard by being so critical and hard on ourselves. Allowing yourself to go downhill only leads you to a life you don't want - a downward spiral that deteriorates your mental and physical well-being. Health and wellness are part of a lifestyle and when you are not right with yourself in the head, your body will reflect that. The Law of Attraction does not lie and a LOST mind leads the body astray. Have the courage to ask yourself, "What have I learned from my traumatic experiences?" Having the courage to recognize your triggers for being unhappy can help you come up with creative self-talk strategies that create a safe space. For example, "This is scary, but I am safe."

The easiest thing we as people do is get tied up in our

thoughts. Some have a better balance on it than others. Learn to listen to what your thoughts are saying rather than get caught up in what's not being said. To balance it all takes practice, patience and compassion. Good news is, it takes 21 days to develop a habit - start with balancing your thoughts.

REFLECTION QUESTION #1 WHAT ARE YOU PASSIONATE ABOUT?

_____
_____
_____
_____
_____
_____
_____
_____
_____
_____
_____
_____
_____
_____
_____
_____
_____
_____
_____
_____

REFLECTION QUESTION # 2
WHAT ARE THE BIGGEST LESSONS YOU'VE LEARNED IN LIFE TO DATE?

_____
_____
_____
_____
_____
_____
_____
_____
_____
_____
_____
_____
_____
_____
_____
_____
_____
_____
_____
_____
_____
_____
_____

REFLECTION QUESTION # 3
WHAT'S THE TOP PRIORITY IN YOUR LIFE RIGHT NOW?

Rising Phoenix

5

Speak it, Write it, Feel it!

"There are no obstacles in your way. Just stairs leading to the next level in your life."

Manifestation, Prayer, Meditation, it all works. I'm a living example - I manifested this book and my whole entrepreneurship. For YEARS I wrote down my thoughts and spoke them out loud and my only issue was that I couldn't feel what I was trying to create. I always felt like there was something in my life that was missing. A true lesson for me was learning that you have two options: fail or succeed. I felt like because I was not truly doing what I loved, I was failing. My aunt who passed away a few years ago once told me, "You have the personality of someone who needs to work for herself."

From there, I knew I had a unique calling.

For about a year and a half, I wrote down how I wanted a particular job. I believed the job was mine so much that I started to say I was already hired and gave myself the title of the job. I did that non-stop for eighteen months. It wasn't until

I finally started to feel that this job was mine that I received an email stating, "You're hired." It was truly magical. I was super excited and believed this was the job for me. However, this job that I wanted so badly was actually preparing me for my own business. Through that job, I learned what not to do, how to treat people who could potentially work for me, or how I like to call it, alongside me.

The Law of Attraction states, "What you think, you create. What you feel, you attract. What you imagine, you become." I wanted to become an entrepreneur and an author, and I felt every bit of this in its existence as though it was in the present. As I write this book, I am speaking of myself as a "Best Selling Author," and by the time you read this book, I will be a best-selling author. In essence, you can create any reality you want, you just have to know which seeds you want to plant.

Imagine having two plants; one is blossoming, with fresh flowers to represent growth, and as you water it, new leaves of creativity, wisdom and knowledge continue to sprout, and the other is wilted and literally on its last leaf, but you keep watering it hoping for a miracle. You eventually realize that because you didn't nurture the wilted plant, it's no longer serving its purpose. Now you have a new pot, fresh seeds, and a chance to learn from your mistakes and start anew. What would you do? Continue to water a dead plant or bring life to a new one? Look at that in terms of your life as a whole and you've got your answer.

TESTIMONY

I PERSONALLY CAN ATTEST to the fact that I lacked confidence and patience for a large part of my life. When I wanted something I would obsess over it and when it didn't happen as expected, I would beat myself up about it. I have to say, with me being called names all of my life, doing the same to myself came easy to me when I would "fail" at something. One day, I saw that I was doing things all wrong. Obsessing over things only blocks blessings from coming into your life. I had to change the pattern by changing the narrative.

I gave myself permission to accept that I was expecting things to happen in my life to reflect what I thought I was missing - happiness. I then changed how I wanted things to come into my life by the power of manifestation. I began to focus on what I really wanted in my life. I was working a low-paying nonprofit job that kept me empty inside, when what I really wanted was something to make me feel worthy and define me.

Fact Check: Living in your true authentic self is what gives you definition and worth, not a job, no matter what it is. The universe has a way of resetting situations in cycles until you catch the wheel before it turns again on your life. I knew that I ultimately had control of how I wanted my experiences to be here on Earth. I wanted to live in a space of love and acceptance of self, and once I started speaking, writing and believing it, my life truly made a 360.

I don't claim to be the expert on life overall, just my own. From my experiences, we bring to life what is watered. It is possible to live in the present and think positively, practically and spiritually into the future. It is possible to be realistic and daydream a little. Whatever it is you think about, you bring life to. The possibilities are endless, depending on your perspective.

REFLECTION QUESTION # 1
WHAT ARE YOU BRINGING TO LIFE AT THE MOMENT?

_____
_____
_____
_____
_____
_____
_____
_____
_____
_____
_____
_____
_____
_____
_____
_____
_____
_____
_____
_____

REFLECTION QUESTION #2
WHAT CHOICES HAVE YOU MADE TO GET THE LIFE YOU DESIRE?

REFLECTION QUESTION #3
WHAT IS YOUR IDEAL LIFE?

_____
_____
_____
_____
_____
_____
_____
_____
_____
_____
_____
_____
_____
_____
_____
_____
_____
_____
_____
_____

DANIELLE RAMIREZ

"I have all that I need. Anything more is just an addition."

- Danielle Ramirez

6

Find Your Tribe, You'll Need Them

"There is not one color that doesn't align right within the rainbow. Be the rainbow and you will attract what aligns."

A strong support system, or as I would like to call it, my tribe, is a huge part of my growth as an entrepreneur. I was lost and unsure of how I could make it as a businesswoman. I had no prior experience and the people I surrounded myself with had no entrepreneurship experience either. Then one day I watched a YouTube segment on Warren Buffet, a successful business owner and mogul; he said that, "You grow in the direction of the people you surround yourself with." MAN! That spoke volumes to me. I then looked around and noticed that my surroundings were in direct conflict with the reality I wanted for myself.

I began to fast. Fasting is another term for getting rid of toxicity from your mind, body and environment. I did this with people, places, and things that were not in alignment with my future. I began to notice how rapidly things began to change, from business owners just showing up in my life, to opportunities coming through the door. I started to be more observant of my current job during this time and started to notice what I did and did not want in my business. I was focused on creating my future and attracting what I wanted to build towards. Before I knew it, I was attracting business grant opportunities and book deals. The opportunities were endless.

What I've learned from my experience and from other entrepreneurs is that you need accountability partners and mentors to help you navigate your journey. You want to get honest feedback from your peers and be open to information that can help you grow and evolve. It is imperative to build your circle during your growth phase. How do you want to grow moving forward? How can you grow into the person you desire to be? I challenge you to ask those questions to your tribe and be enlightened in many forms.

Here's another fact check: not everyone is meant to move on with you to the next phase of your journey in life. Your new life will come with sacrifices, but also rewards. It is up to you to choose the path that gives you the most growth.

REFLECTION QUESTION # 1
WHAT CAN I DO TO MOTIVATE MYSELF TO ACCOMPLISH GOALS THIS YEAR?

_____
_____
_____
_____
_____
_____
_____
_____
_____
_____
_____
_____
_____
_____
_____
_____
_____
_____
_____
_____

REFLECTION QUESTION # 2
HOW IS SOMEONE PART OF MY GROWTH?

_____
_____
_____
_____
_____
_____
_____
_____
_____
_____
_____
_____
_____
_____
_____
_____
_____
_____
_____
_____

REFLECTION QUESTION # 3
WHO IS NOT A PART OF MY GROWTH? AND WHY?

Rising Phoenix

7

Who Are You? Really?

"A flower doesn't stop growing because the other flowers haven't caught up. Be the flower that doesn't stop growing."

Learning myself was the hardest part of my journey. I was not sure who I was when I looked in the mirror and I wasn't sure if I was ready to find out. I had lived years wearing what I believed was a mask of different personalities that seemed to fit at the time, but when I removed them, I was a different person. I learned quickly that your mind will believe everything you tell it. If you feed it hate, you will believe it, but if you feed it love, you will learn love. I had family members and friends who knew me better than I knew myself. I was walking around blind about who I had become and letting my skills and passion fall by the wayside. Then I asked myself, who am I?

I worked hard on finding out who I wanted to become by rediscovering who I was to begin with. I started listening to music that raised my vibration and gave me clarity. I focused on what made me happy and invested in that! I discovered old habits I needed to get rid of, like judging and feeling sorry for myself. From those intimate conversations with myself, I discovered that it's okay. You just forgot you who were for a little while. Welcome back.

Finding yourself can come with some resistance. You will have people who doubt your growth and only remember the person you were instead of looking at the person you have grown to be. You also will go through a phase where you yourself will doubt the journey. Eventually there will be a disconnect from the people who you thought were your friends and even some family members. What I discovered along the way is that it doesn't matter what anyone thinks of you. If you continue to worry about how you are perceived, you will continue to live a life based on other people's opinions. Eliminating the impulse to people please is where the true growth transformation and healing process begins. You'll start to think, am I doing this right? Did I give up on people? What is happening? Am I who I think I am? All these questions are just some of what you will be asking yourself. Trust me, it is okay and all you need to do is trust the process and keep going.

I encourage you to take a break from it all and learn who you are and what brings you joy. I always tell people that if it doesn't bring you joy, don't do it. You are your biggest supporter and the only person who can love, be kind and make improvements on yourself. From experience, if you can master self, anything after that is a piece of cake. You will become this new motivated and brilliant being that will attract abundance in its purest form. Like attracts like and if you are not seeing a true reflection of yourself in your surroundings, dig deep, reflect, release and build anew. You will thank me later.

Every person has a certain image of you that makes them

comfortable with who you are. Once you outgrow that image and become more than they were comfortable with, it makes them confused, unsettled and jealous, because now either they themselves have to grow or they'll want you to shrink back to fit their expectation. Never shrink back. Keep growing.

REFLECTION QUESTION #1
WHICH 3 WORDS DESCRIBE ME BEST?

_____
_____
_____
_____
_____
_____
_____
_____
_____
_____
_____
_____
_____
_____
_____
_____
_____
_____
_____
_____
_____

REFLECTION QUESTION #2
HOW CAN I CHALLENGE MYSELF MORE?

REFLECTION QUESTION #3
WHAT ARE MY PERSONAL GIFTS?

_____
_____
_____
_____
_____
_____
_____
_____
_____
_____
_____
_____
_____
_____
_____
_____
_____
_____
_____
_____

DANIELLE RAMIREZ

8

Say NO to Doubt

"One thing about going down the wrong path is that you can always turn around."

Here I am at a place in life where I relied on myself to solve problems and figure things out. I would be ashamed to ask for help because others always relied on me to be their source of help. I would ask myself, "How could I possibly help others if I can't help myself?" This is where I had to dig deep and submit to the divine, universe and GOD in order to trust what was happening around me. I've always admired people who have a "go with the flow" type of approach to life. They are attuned to the present and pretty much took each situation in stride. I, on the other hand, would have a need-to-control-everything-around-me approach. There's that childhood trauma creeping in. A time where I felt I was not in control led me to want to have too much control in my adult life.

I want you to be prepared for when doubt surfaces, because your subconscious will need you to affirm your belief that you are trusting for all things to align. The ability to transmute energy that is low vibrational and leaves you stagnant into energies that can serve you in a good way is a powerful skill to have. When you evolve, you will go through a shift that involves shedding an old version of you that is not in alignment with the new person you are becoming. The old version of you perhaps didn't take chances, didn't step out of your comfort zone or take risks. The old version of you perhaps didn't believe in the person you could become. This is when trusting the process and releasing all doubts leads to growth.

When in doubt, there are three key things to keep in mind. (1) Meditate: Write down exactly what you want and surround your-self with others who can motivate you toward your dream/ goals. Mediation (or prayer) is a process where you dig deep and focus on exactly what you want. Visualize how this will help you down to the specifics. For example, some may say, "I want a new car," but when that new car arrives, you are not able to afford it or it's not as reliable as you thought it would be. So a way to visualize the specifics is to say, "I want a new car that I can afford monthly payments on, that will not stretch my finances thin and is reliable." (2) Create your vision: Let your environment become a reflection of the reality you want. For example, surround your home or work space with things that spark your creativity and enhance your vibration, i.e., plants, music, motivational words. Let your soul and vibration impact your external reality. (3) Be Visual: When I was looking for a job, I purchased clothing that I would wear once I was hired. I have heard of women who desire to have children and would buy small baby items to bring forth their vision into reality. Most people nowadays believe the majority of what they see. When you believe in yourself and visualize your best self, you ultimately create your future reality. The specifics are going to allow you to clearly write down your goals and desires, which in turn will bring the proper surroundings to your life.

As discussed in earlier chapters, you want your team, circle and close relationships to be solid. However, the goal is to be grounded and solid in your own right. Although your support system will be inspirational in uplifting you and bring out your most successful qualities, the take-away of this chapter is to become confident in the person you're becoming while also building your starting five. Like in basketball, you want winners on your team, but the Coach (you) brings it all together.

REFLECTION QUESTION #1
WHO ARE YOU TODAY COMPARED TO WHO YOU WERE FIVE YEARS AGO?

_____
_____
_____
_____
_____
_____
_____
_____
_____
_____
_____
_____
_____
_____
_____
_____
_____
_____
_____
_____

REFLECTION QUESTION # 2
WHAT IS YOUR BIGGEST TAKEAWAY IN LIFE TO DATE?

_____
_____
_____
_____
_____
_____
_____
_____
_____
_____
_____
_____
_____
_____
_____
_____
_____
_____
_____
_____
_____
_____

REFLECTION QUESTION # 3
IF YOU COULD GIVE YOURSELF ANY ADVICE, WHAT WOULD IT BE?

Rising Phoenix

9

Stay True to You

"Stop waiting on permission to go after what you want in life."

This chapter is one of the most important lessons I learned in life. When I talk about staying true to who you are, I am talking about coming into the "you" phase. Success can cause people to wear different masks that are not a true representation of self. Sometimes we tend to camouflage within certain surroundings for the sake of "fitting in" with society and their views. When you are your true authentic self, there is no need to adjust yourself for others. I also struggled with knowing who my true self was because for the majority of my life, I was living a life others wanted me to live. I had no true identity and when I looked in the mirror, I was unrecognizable.

As an entrepreneur, I learned the significance of knowing what your identity is and to live in your truth. My business is a reflection of me. In chapter one, I discussed how to find yourself. There are no imperfections or perfections, you are who you are. Be proud of it. I turned out to be the greater amount of who I needed to be by finding what it was I deeply desired. As you continue to develop, your point of view of yourself will change. For me, it was understanding my worth that turned into the establishment for building my future.

The most important lesson I hope you learn from this book is to always choose yourself when others do not. Learn to understand who you are and own every part of you. Discover and rediscover. Evaluate and re-evaluate. Learn how your energy reacts to people, places and certain environments. When you operate in a state of learning, you take chances on yourself and learn to never underestimate your own potential. Operate from a space of gratitude and you will never be without inner fulfillment. When you have inner fulfillment, you come into your own power and can literally create the life you want, even during a global pandemic.

The best thing for your personal and professional growth is to stay true to you. In a world with so many lost souls, you can't afford to be lost yourself. What this book has to offer is hope. Hope is what you will need to believe in the impossible. Whatever goals you want to build for yourself, do it. It is time to start becoming more confident and to stop underestimating your potential. It's the person you never saw coming that will change your life, and that person will be you.

REFLECTION QUESTION # 1
WHERE DO YOU GO FROM HERE?

REFLECTION QUESTION # 2
WHAT DOES THE NEXT CHAPTER OF YOUR LIFE LOOK LIKE?

_____
_____
_____
_____
_____
_____
_____
_____
_____
_____
_____
_____
_____
_____
_____
_____
_____
_____
_____
_____
_____

REFLECTION QUESTION # 3
WHAT DO I NEED TO CHANGE ABOUT MYSELF?

_____
_____
_____
_____
_____
_____
_____
_____
_____
_____
_____
_____
_____
_____
_____
_____
_____
_____
_____
_____
_____
_____

Rising Phoenix

10

Growth

"Your story will be someone else's survival guide."

Growth is ground-breaking. You are continually developing regardless of the circumstance or situation. Be that as it may, each developing period presents a lesson. It's imperative to be mindful of those lessons since that is the genuine meaning of growth - the capacity to comprehend why certain encounters occur throughout everyday life and that within each hardship is a silver lining. I am a firm believer that every person has a story and if we pay attention to those chapters in our story, we will see how far we have come and where we are headed.

Your growth will help you change toxic patterns into healthy behaviors, your wounds will heal, you will be empowered to heal others because before you decide to serve others you must know what you are lacking. I think some people believe that personal growth should come easily, but in reality this is not how the Law of Attraction works. Life is about lessons, and those lessons allow you to build awareness and with each awareness comes a higher level of maturity and wisdom. As children, we observe and absorb our environment and the people in it. As we grow and become more established, a similar concept applies, yet now you are more capable of making conscious choices on whom and what you absorb while still observing.

Let your growth be your motivation to do better and allow better around you. Honestly speaking, with growth, like a tree growing, there will be some weeds and dead leaves that fall by the wayside. Those weeds and dead leaves are your old life and old habits that no longer serve you. People from that life will also try to project their beliefs and experiences onto you. Some of those people will be your family and some of the closet people in your life. Whenever you find yourself in the midst of these experiences, always remind yourself to use your negative experiences and turn them into positive ones. With awareness comes a certain understanding that not everyone is meant to be a part of your journey and some experiences and people come into our lives for a season and a reason.

TESTIMONY

2020 HANDED ME a butt kicking like no other. There were many times prior to 2020 in my life that I wasn't paying attention to what the universe was showing me. Toxic patterns kept repeating, relationships that had passed their expiration date, and the excess baggage my inner being was carrying blocked my blessings. These things weren't conducive to the life I wanted for myself. In the process of my transformation and rebirth, I realized very quickly that the people that are meant to be in my life will always be there, but as I dealt with milestones and bad experiences, I learned the value of the greatest relationship of all, the relationship with self. I have to admit, I was devastated by the ending of some relationships and wasn't surprised by the betrayal by others. I was taken for granted, used and abused; others projected their traumas onto me and I allowed it all to happen at the expense of wanting people in my life. The biggest life lesson for me was understanding the difference between loyalty and love.

I cherished individuals who weren't loyal to me and honestly the type of "love" I was receiving from these individuals was not what I needed in my life. Their form of love was to call me names, belittle me, envy me, and most of all, be hurtful with their actions. For some time, I took ownership of all those attacks as though it was my responsibility, when my main job was to claim my own reality. My growth through the awful encounters permitted me to use sound judgment and allow positives to fulfill my life. My circumstances did not define me, but rather helped my inner being become more insightful, and adjust and adapt what I had learned through those experiences.

In order to gain my peace, I had to stop not only arguing with people but also accepting and excusing toxic behaviors simply because acceptance was more comfortable than change. Without those pivotal points in my life, I wouldn't be where I am now.

There comes a time when you have to not let the actions of others impact your moral compass. You also have to take accountability and responsibility for the choices you make in life. Just because you developed an awareness doesn't mean you have a pass to still exhibit the same behaviors and expect different results. One thing about growth is that it comes in many forms. Being able to recognize how inner growth is just as important as outer growth is where true wisdom from the lessons emerges.

REFLECTION QUESTION # 1
AM I HOLDING ONTO SOMETHING I NEED TO LET GO OF?

_____
_____
_____
_____
_____
_____
_____
_____
_____
_____
_____
_____
_____
_____
_____
_____
_____
_____
_____
_____

REFLECTION QUESTION # 2
WHAT AM I DOING ABOUT THE THINGS THAT MATTER MOST IN MY LIFE?

REFLECTION QUESTION # 3
IF YOU COULD WRITE THE 11th STEP TO THIS BOOK, WHAT WOULD THAT BE AND WHY?

_____
_____
_____
_____
_____
_____
_____
_____
_____
_____
_____
_____
_____
_____
_____
_____
_____
_____
_____
_____

DANIELLE RAMIREZ

Epilogue

So what if I didn't write this book? What if I didn't take a chance on myself? What if I never gave myself what I deserved? Well, this book wouldn't be here and you wouldn't be here reading this guide. Earlier in the book I wrote, "A flower doesn't stop growing because others haven't caught up." My advice is to wait for no one. The goal of this book is to help you be the flower that doesn't stop growing. Most importantly, love yourself wholeheartedly because no one else can or should fulfill that role but you. So I challenge you to gain insight into who you are and where you're going. The key to a better life is to go after it!

YOU'RE THE INSPIRATION. Be inspired.

IF YOU ARE SEEKING to remove any roadblocks you are currently experiencing in your life, let me travel on the path of change with you so that you can tap into your full potential in achieving your goals. You are in control as you rise to your own light and watch yourself enjoy life. I will partner with you to help you accomplish what means the most to you. Most importantly, you will establish the belief that CHANGE IS POSSIBLE.

YOUR COACHING EXPERIENCE with Danielle at Phoenix Rising Coaching Services, LLC

TAKE a moment today and ask yourself if you are living the life you truly deserve. Do you love yourself with full acceptance? If you feel you are challenged with developmental areas in your life, let's explore together. As your coach, I will focus on you without judgment. I work with a variety of individuals who desire flexible, measurable and achievable goals. What sets me apart from other coaches is that I am a certified professional coach trained and gifted in sharing my light of peace, love, joy and partnering with you on identifying what real happiness means to you. Here at Phoenix Rising, I follow a C-A-R-E designed method; its purpose is to build Confidence, Acceptance, Reassurance and Elevation in each and every individual.

About the Author

Danielle Ramirez is a Certified Professional Life Coach who specializes in Personal Development Coaching with a Solution-Focused approach. She has a background in Clinical Mental Health Counseling and is a Veteran of the U.S. Army. Danielle started her coaching career in 2018 with the goal in mind to help women overcome and heal their trauma and build their future with confidence. Her motto is "Feelings Change. Self-Worth and Respect Shouldn't." Danielle's accreditation is through the International Coaching Federation (ICF) where she holds certification as an Associate Certified Coach (ACC).

Danielle set out and began her coaching business Phoenix Rising Coaching Services, LLC at a time when she was embarking on her personal discovery journey of solution-building and walking in her purpose. Throughout this journey, she tapped into her own potential within the coaching profession and immediately fell in love with the profession of having compassion, partnership, acceptance, and a style of conversation that was true to the individual. She then set out to have Phoenix Rising represent transition and rebirth. She mentions how life, like the phoenix bird, signifies coming into a new version of yourself and taking flight to become the person you are destined to be. Danielle's journey as a phoenix is truly liberating, enlightening and free. As a life coach, she shares some of her greatest experiences in hopes to enlighten and empower her audience. She watches her clients explore their own freedom as well as their ability to discover, design, manifest, and deliver change within their life.

Danielle has developed a guide to learn more about herself, her independence and her desired goals. Most importantly, she shares those teachings with the belief that CHANGE IS POSSIBLE.

Connect with Danielle Ramirez on Social Media

Follow me via Facebook: Phoenix Rising Coaching
Follow me via Instagram: @phoenixrisingcoachingservices
Phoenix Rising Coaching Services, LLC
www.phoenixrisingcoachingservices.com

www.ingramcontent.com/pod-product-compliance
Lightning Source LLC
Chambersburg PA
CBHW070741230426
43669CB00014B/2535